HOLINESS

AS UNDERSTOOD BY

THE WRITERS OF THE BIBLE.

A BIBLE STUDY.

BY

JOSEPH AGAR BEET.

"Give what Thou bid'st: and bid what Thou wilt."—AUGUSTINE.

ISBN 0-88019-174-0

Schmul Publishing Co., Inc.
Wesleyan Book Club   1985   Salem, Ohio

Printed by
Old Paths Tract Society Inc.
Shoals, Indiana 47581

PREFACE TO THE FIRST EDITION.

———•———

THIS small work is designed both for students of the original Scriptures and for readers of the English Bible. It will be useful chiefly to those who will test my opinions by searching out and studying for themselves the passages from which they have been derived. A few paragraphs designed only for those acquainted with the sacred languages, and printed in smaller type, will be easily passed over by the general reader. May God grant that the study of this subject be as profitable to my readers as it has been to myself.

JOSEPH AGAR BEET.

STAFFORD, *February* 11, 1880.

PREFACE TO THE SECOND EDITION.

————•————

THE present edition is a corrected reprint of the former one. That my exposition of the holiness of God has encountered considerable objection from reviewers in no wise surprises me. The differences of opinion among the best scholars prompted me to speak with caution (page 19) on so difficult a subject. Of these differences a conspicuous example is found in the new edition of Herzog's *Encyclopedia*, in two papers side by side from the pens of Delitsch and Lange.

I notice, however, that my critics do not discuss the reasons for my exposition, given on pages 19, 27, 29, 34, 45. One reviewer contents himself with saying that he has "been accustomed to regard God's holiness as implying, first of all, the absence from the Divine mind of every principle which would involve moral imperfection; secondly, the possession of all the principles and affections which are suited to the relations in which God stands to his creatures, and which are included in moral rectitude and, thirdly, an intense delight in that which is morally pure and good, and a hatred to every thing morally evil;" and in support of this view quotes an able work on systematic theology.

Against the treatment which this subject has received in most such works I must raise a serious protest. For the more part writers have contented themselves with assuming, without any proof or any reference to the 'great difficulty of the subject, a meaning for the word holy when predicated of God, and have then expounded their own arbitrary interpretation. But the truths conveyed by Bible words can be learned only by a careful search for the idea which lies at the root of the entire Bible use of them. In the Old Testament the idea of holiness is inseparably linked to the Mosaic ritual. And this must therefore be the point of departure of all investigation into the holiness of God. But the path which leads from this starting-point to the goal reached by the reviewer quoted above I am unable to trace.

The arbitrary selection of meanings for Bible words has been hitherto the disgrace of systematic theology. It is one chief cause of the present comparative neglect of this all-important study, by making it appear to be nothing else but a series of unproved assertions. This disgrace is, however, being rapidly rolled away.

The foregoing reply has no reference to a courteous critic, who, in the *United Presbyterian Magazine*, endeavors to vindicate for the holiness of God the idea of separation from sin. But this idea is not nearly so closely connected with that embodied in the Mosaic ritual as is the exposition I have adopted. And in the Bible the ritual conception of holiness is never out of sight.

An interesting passage, illustrative of the radical idea of holiness, but hitherto overlooked by me, is Deut. xxii, 9: "Thou shalt not sow thy vineyard with two different things, lest the fruit of thy seed be sanctified " —that is, lest it be forfeited to God. This harmonizes completely with the conception unfolded in the following pages.

I cannot forbear to express my thankfulness for the reception given to this work by men of all churches, on both sides of the Atlantic, and even in the Southern Hemisphere. I take it as pleasant proof that my researches in this all-important subject have not been in vain.

WARRINGTON, *September* 23, 1880.

CONTENTS.

HOLINESS,

AS UNDERSTOOD BY THE WRITERS OF THE BIBLE.

———•———

SECTION I.

METHOD OF STUDY.

I SHALL attempt to set forth in this little book, as correctly and fully as I can, the teaching of the Bible about HOLINESS.

In order to do this it will be needful to determine first what the writers of the Bible meant by this word; for it is both an ancient and a modern word. And, unless we understand it in the sense in which it was used by Moses, the prophets, and the apostles, we shall be in danger of putting into their writings a meaning far from their intention, a meaning derived from modern religious life and thought; and we shall certainly lose much of the truth their words were designed to convey. This need to study the meaning of Bible words marks a difference between theology and nearly all other branches of human knowledge, In most of these we may ourselves choose the sense of our own terms. And, if the sense be clearly defined and maintained throughout, no confusion or error arises. But the words of the Bible are not ours, but God's. And they existed and had a definite meaning in the minds of the sacred writers long before men thought of systematic theology. This meaning we must therefore reverently and patiently search for and keep in mind while we study the matters of which they wrote.

But how can we determine the meaning of these sacred words? Just as in childhood we learned the meaning of the words of our mother tongue. We then observed the various concrete objects for which they were used; we noticed the qualities common to the objects called by the same name; and thus, by the inborn power of abstraction, we formed a conception of the idea conveyed by the name. And in this way the conception of holiness must have been formed in the mind of ancient Israel. We will, therefore, as we pass along through the pages of holy Scripture, observe the various objects called holy and the various connections of thought in which the word holy occurs; and we will try to find out the one idea embodied in these various objects and conveyed by the one word used to designate all. We shall thus place ourselves as nearly as possible in the position of the earliest people we know of who used the word holy, and shall learn its meaning as they did.

This method of study has another advantage. As we pass along the ages of the Bible we shall find that the conception of holiness becomes deeper and broader. We shall observe that successive revelations of truth, far from setting aside this old word and finding a new one, gave to it a fresh significance and a broader application. We shall thus, by our consecutive study of holy Scripture, be able to trace this development of the conception of holiness as the ages of the old covenant roll by until the full glory of holiness is revealed in the person of Jesus Christ the Holy One of God. In this way, while tracing the meaning of one of the most important words of the Bible, we shall really trace the progress of God's revelation of himself to man.

Before proceeding further it will be well to say that in both Testaments the words holy, hallow, holiness, correspond exactly to saint, sanctify, sanctification. These words may be transposed without error. A saint is a holy person ; holiness is the state resulting from the act of sanctification. That we have two families of words for one idea results from the fact that our language is a Latin superstructure built upon a German foundation. From each of these languages we derive words conveying the one idea of holiness.

SECTION II.

HOLINESS IN THE BOOKS OF THE LAW.

ALL theological words belonged originally to secular life. They were born on profane soil and were servants once of the common things of common life. Usually, therefore, our study of Bible words begins with an attempt to determine their original secular significance.

Such a significance, doubtless, the word holy once had. But it has become altogether undistinguishable in the early twilight of history. For when called to enter the service of religion this work forsook entirely the associations of its earlier life, and was invested with a new significance which occupied it so completely that of its supposed earlier significance no certain trace remains. Wherever found it has reference to religion.

Our inability to trace the genealogy of the word is, however, little or no loss. For at the Exodus the word came suddenly into very common use, like the word "photograph" in our own day, to denote a new conception, an offspring of a new revelation from God. And it was at once applied to objects so many and so various, and henceforth so familiar to the eyes and thought of Israel, that by means of these objects its meaning must have been clearly and accurately, though perhaps unconsciously, defined in the mind of every Israelite. And as they learned its meaning from familiar and visible objects so we may learn it from the books of the law, which give us a full description of these objects.

It is very significant that in Genesis the word holy never occurs; sanctify only once—in a passage which probably received its literary form from the voice of Sinai. And the reason is not far to seek. The idea of holiness was not revealed definitely to man until the time of Moses. And it was one of the most conspicuous features of the Mosaic covenant, as the word which conveys it is the most conspicuous word in the books in which that covenant is recorded. The one passage in Genesis in which the word sanctify is found, and two cognate words which cast some light upon the essential idea of holiness, we will refer to again.

We must therefore begin our study of holiness by searching the four books which contain the Mosaic covenant. Our search is soon rewarded. In the solemn opening scene of that covenant, from the lips of God, and in a connection of thought wonderfully indicative of the nature of the covenant he had come down to make, we hear for the first time the great word henceforth to be so deeply interwoven with the religious life of Israel and of mankind. God's words to Moses from the bush, " Draw not nigh hither; for the ground which thou art standing upon is ground of holiness," Exod. iii, 5, introduce a covenant of which one great feature was to be holiness embodied in visible places and things; a holiness which made the holy objects partly or altogether inaccessible to man. The meaning of the word in this passage is clear. God meant to say that the ground stood in special relation to himself, and that because it was God's ground none could tread it except by his command.

We next meet with the word in Exod. xii, 16—convocation of holiness. This was evidently a calling together of the people which had special reference to God—that is, not for some secular purpose, but at the bidding of God and to work out his purpose.

Very instructive for determining the sense of the word holy are the words of Exod. xiii, 2, " Sanctify to me the first-born." For they are explained at once by the words, " It is mine ; " and by v. 12, " Thou shalt make all that open the womb pass over to Jehovah : the males are Jehovah's." With this compare Num. iii, 12, 13, " I have taken the Levites from among the sons of Israel instead of all the first-born from the sons of Israel : and the Levites shall be mine. For mine are all the first-born. For in the day when I smote all the first-born in Egypt I sanctified for myself every first-born in Israel, from man to beast. Mine shall they be." Also Num. viii, 16, 17, " They are altogether given to me from among the sons of Israel. Instead of such as open every womb, even every first-born from the sons of Israel, I have taken them for myself." And Deut. xv, 19, " Every first-born male thou shalt sanctify to Jehovah thy God : thou shalt do no work with the first-born of thine ox, nor shear the first-born of thy sheep." These passages make quite clear the meaning of the word sanctify in Exod. xiii, 2. The first-born were to be holy in the sense that they were to stand in a special relation to God as his property, and were to be touched by man only according to the bidding and to work out the purposes of God. In other words, they were not man's, but God's.

In Exod. xv, 11, God is said to be " glorious in holiness ; " and in ver. 13 we read of the " dwelling-place of thy holiness." But these verses do not, taken by themselves, throw much light upon the central idea of holiness. We shall therefore reserve them till we have completed our study of the Mosaic ritual.

The solemn words of Exod. xix, 6, " Ye shall be to me a kingdom of priests, a holy nation," are especially important as illustrating the meaning of the word holy, because of their contrast with Exod. xiii, 2. They are explained by the foregoing words, " Ye shall be a peculiar treasure to me above all people : for all the earth is mine ; " of which the phrase " a holy nation " is evidently a summing up. And, by the words " kingdom of priests," the word holy is linked with the ritual soon to be established. Just as in Egypt God had already declared that the first-born should stand in special relation to himself as his property, in virtue of their deliverance from the destroyer, so now he says that the entire nation shall stand in a similar, though perhaps not exactly the same, relation to himself, in virtue (ver. 4) of its deliverance from Egypt. Thus we have in this passage an anticipation of the holiness which now belongs to every

member of the Church of Christ. The same wider use
of the word is found in Lev. xi, 44, 45 ; xx, 26. In these
two last passages we find mention of subjective holiness ;
of which we shall say more at the end of this section.
To men already claimed by God to be his own, and in
that sense already holy, God declares that they " shall be
holy "—that is, that they shall render to him the devotion
he requires.

The words of Exod. xix, 23, " Set bounds around the
mountain and sanctify it," develop chap. iii, 5. By putting a fence Moses marked off the mountain as belonging
to God, and therefore not to be trodden by man or beast
except at his bidding.

And now, beneath the shadow of the holy mountain,
rises before us the complicated solemnity of the Mosaic
ritual ; and of that ritual every vessel and every rite
bears on its front, in broad and deep characters, the
name of " Holiness." The tabernacle is called the
" Sanctuary " or holy place. Exod. xxv, 8. The outer
chamber bears the abstract title, " holiness ; " the inner
one bears the superlative name, " holiness of holinesses,"
conveniently rendered in our version, " holy of holies,"
chap. xxvi, 33. The same august superlative title is
given in chap. xxix, 37, to the brazen altar ; in chap.
xxx, 29, to the vessels of the tabernacle ; and in Lev.
ii, 3, to the bodies of animals offered in sacrifice. In the
last passage it is explained by the words, " The remnant
from the meat-offering is for Aaron and for his sons : it
is holy of holies from the burnings of Jehovah." In

other words, the unburnt parts of the sacrifices were
God's, and were therefore to be given to the priests, his
servants.   So absolute was the holiness of these sacred
objects that God said three times, Exod. xxix, 37;
xxx, 29; Lev. vi, 18, "Whatever touches the altar shall
be holy"—that is, by that touch it ceases to be man's
possession and must henceforth be used only for the
purposes of God.   Aaron and his clothes, and his sons
and their clothes, were holy. Exod. xxix, 21. So was
the oil: "Upon man's flesh it shall not be poured, neither
shall ye make any like it: it is holy, and shall be holy to
you. Whoever compounds any like it, and whoever puts
any of it upon a stranger, shall even be cut off from his
people." Exod. xxx, 32.   Houses, fields, and cattle,
were made holy by consecration to God. Lev. xxvii,
9, 14. Their holiness is thus described in ver. 21: "The
field shall be holy for Jehovah, like the field of the
anathema: for the priest the possession of it shall be."
If a man wanted back something he had sanctified he
must pay for it. Ver. 15.   But some objects were given
to God by an irrevocable consecration, and were called
"anathema," and "holy of holies. Vers. 28, 29.   The
Nazarite was holy, Num. vi, 5, 8; and his sacrifice was
"holiness for the priest," ver. 20. The censers of Korah
were holy, Num. xvi, 38, and therefore could not be put
to common use. The fourth year's fruit of the land of
Canaan was holy.   Lev. xix, 24.   The Sabbath is called
holy: "Whoever does any work therein shall be cut off
from his people."   Exod. xxxi, 14. Lastly, God says to

Israel in Deut. vii, 6, "A holy people thou art for Jehovah thy God: thee has Jehovah thy God chosen to be
his, for a people of special possession beyond all the
peoples which are upon the face of the earth."

The above passages from the books of the law are
samples of hundreds of others. In all of them the
meaning is the same, and is clearly marked. These holy
objects stand in a special relation to God as his property.
Consequently they are not man's. They have no human
owner who can do with them as he pleases. None can
touch them except at the bidding of God. Else, as we
learn from Mal. iii, 8, they will be guilty of robbing God.
The word holiness is the inviolable broad-arrow of the
divine King of Israel.

We are told in Num. iii, 13, Exod. xxix, 44, xx, 11,
Lev. xxii, 32, that it was God who sanctified the first-
born, the tabernacle and altar, and Aaron and his sons,
the Sabbath and the people. For the devotion of these
objects to God originated not in man, but in God. With
very few limited exceptions nothing could be given to
God but what he had first claimed for himself.

Moses also, as the minister through whom the devotion to God of these objects was brought about, is said
in Exod. xix, 14, xxviii, 41, xxix, 1, xl, 9–13, to have
sanctified Mount Sinai, Aaron, and the tabernacle and its
vessels.

Since some of the objects claimed by God were themselves intelligent beings, and others were in the control
of such beings, their devotion to God could take place

only by man's consent. Consequently the priests and the people are said in Exod. xix, 22, Lev. xi, 44, xxvii, 14, to sanctify themselves and some of their possessions. They did this either by formally placing themselves or their goods at the disposal of God or by separating themselves from whatever was inconsistent with the service of God. Hence holiness implied renunciation of idolatry and of meats pronounced unclean. Lev. xx, 7; xxi, 4; xx, 25; xxi, 1–8.

Already, in Exod. xv, 11, 13, Moses has sung of God as "glorious in holiness," and of the "dwelling-place of his holiness." And in four passages, Lev. xi, 45; xix, 2; xx, 26; xxi, 8, God solemnly declares that he is himself holy; and on the ground of his own holiness commands the people to sanctify themselves and to be holy. In two of these passages the holiness of God is given as a reason for abstaining from unclean food; a third passage has reference to the holiness of the priests; and another is a warning to honor parents, to keep the Sabbath, and to turn from idolatry. In Lev. x, 3, God declares, "In those who are near to me I will be sanctified: and in the presence of all the people I will be glorified." Similarly, Num. xx, 12; xxvii, 14; Deut. xxxii, 51. Also Lev. xxii, 32: "And ye shall not profane the name of my holiness: and I will be sanctified in the midst of the sons of Israel; I am Jehovah, your sanctifier; who brought you forth from the land of Egypt, to be to you a God."

To determine the precise sense in which in these

passages God declares that he is holy is no easy task. Of this a clear proof is found in the widely-different expositions of them given by the ablest scholars. It therefore becomes me to speak with caution.

One thing, however, is certain. In the four passages in which God speaks of himself as holy, all which are found in the book which treats specially of the Levitical ritual, and in the two passages quoted above from the song of Moses, and in the passages in which God claims to be sanctified by those who surround him, the word holy must represent the same idea as in the hundreds of passages surrounding them in the books of the law in which it is predicated of men and things. For the number and commonness and variety of the concrete and visible objects called holy in the every-day life of Israel must have given to the word a clearly-defined meaning well understood by every Israelite. By predicating the word of himself God declared plainly that these holy objects set forth one of his own attributes. This is not disproved by the fact that the word could not be spoken of God in precisely the same sense as of man. For an idea may be the same although its relation to the object in which it is embodied be different. Just so, when we speak of people as healthy, and from this infer that their home is healthy, we express by the word "healthy" the same idea, although differently embodied in a healthy man and a healthy place. We therefore ask, What new view of God did Israel obtain by contemplating these various holy objects, rational

and irrational? In them we must seek for a manifestation of an attribute of God, an attribute bearing to
these created holy objects a relation similar to that of
the Creator to the creature.

We have seen that holiness is God's claim to the
ownership and the exclusive use of various men, things,
and portions of time, and that the objects claimed were
called holy. Now God's claim was a new and wonderful
revelation of his nature. Moses, Aaron, and Israel, as
they encamped around the sacred tent, had thoughts
of God very different from their thoughts in former days.
To Aaron God was now the great Being who had
claimed from him a life-long and exclusive service.
This claim was a new era, not only in his every-day life,
but in his conception of God. Consequently the word
holy, which expressed Aaron's relation to God, was suitably used to express God's relation to Aaron. In other
words, to Aaron and Israel God was holy in the sense
that he claimed the exclusive ownership and use of the
various holy objects, and thus claimed virtually and
practically the ownership of the entire nation. "Ye
shall be to me holy men: for holy am I, Jehovah. And
I have separated you from the nations to be mine."
Lev. xx, 26. Since God's claim to the absolute devotion
of his people surpasses infinitely every claim ever put
forth on behalf of the gods of heathendom, it reveals
the majesty of God. And, in Exod. xv, 11, Moses could
appropriately sing, "Who is like thee among the gods,
glorious in holiness?" Mount Sinai, since there God sol-

emnly announced his claim, was fitly called in ver. 13, "The dwelling-place of thy holiness." When God manifested, by word or act, the strictness of his claim, he was said to be sanctified, as in Lev. x, 3, in the case of Nadab and Abihu. When men yielded to God the devotion he claimed—that is, when in the subjective world of their own inner and outer life they put God in the place of honor as their Master and Owner, they were said to sanctify God. So Deut. xxxii, 51; Num. xxvii, 14, "Because ye sanctified me not in the midst of Israel."

We notice in passing that the holiness both of God and of man is set forth in the old covenant only in symbolic outline. For a complete conception of it we must wait till in the face of Jesus Christ we see the full glory of God.

We have now learned, by a study of the four later books of the law, as every Israelite must have learned far more thoroughly from objects around him, that holiness is God's claim to the proprietorship and use of certain objects; and we have found the word holy predicated both of the objects claimed and of him who claimed them. We notice also that God's claim put a broad separation between these objects and all others, and erected an inviolable barrier between the holy things and the mass of the nation.

From this point we will look back upon the book of Genesis. It is as likely as not that the one passage, ii, 3, "God sanctified the seventh day," was written after the

giving of the law, and, if so, it may have taken its form
from Exod. xx, 11. The words, " And God blessed the
seventh day," seem to teach that at the creation God
pronounced this blessing. And if so looked upon in the
light of Exod. xx, 11, " Jehovah blessed the seventh day
and sanctified it," that blessing might be spoken of as
sanctification of the seventh day. But this is imma-
terial. The sense here is exactly the same as that de-
termined above. God claimed the day to be specially
his own. So Isa. lviii, 13: "Turn away thy foot from
the sabbath, from doing thy pleasure on my day of
holiness."

In Gen. xxxviii, 21, as in Deut. xxiii, 17, a cognate
word is used to designate a profligate woman. This recalls the " sacred slave-girls " at Corinth " whom both
men and women presented to the goddess." Strabo
vii, 378. The essential idea of holiness is found here,
though in a peculiar form. Devotion to an impure deity
creates impurity in the devotee ; whereas devotion to
God implies separation from all impurity.

Another trace of the word is found in the name
Kadesh, in Gen. xiv, 7; xvi, 14; xx, 1. This name, also
given to other towns in Josh. xx, 7 (xv, 23) ; 1 Chr. vi, 72,
suggests that the towns which bore it were specially devoted to the service of some deity. We may compare
the Greek name, Hieropolis, of a city in Phrygia noted
for its temple of Cybele, and of another in the north-east
of Syria, a chief seat of the worship of Astarte.

We see then that the use of the word holy in Genesis

confirms the results obtained by our study of the four later books of the law. And this confirmation is the more valuable because of the total dissimilarity of the surroundings of the words.

Thus from the earliest writings of the Bible we have gathered a clear conception of holiness as understood in the early morning of the sacred nation. And the correctness of our conception is vouched for by the abundant use of the word in the books of the law and by the great variety of the objects to which it is applied.

An independent confirmation of the same is found in an inscription from Cyprus in two languages, Phœnician and Greek, in which יקדש is translated by ἀνέθηκεν.* The total difference of the source of this inscription from that of the Hebrew Scriptures gives great value to its agreement with them in the conception of holiness.

---

* Quoted in a very instructive and interesting book, *Biblical and Oriental Studies*, p. 347. By W. Turner, of Edinburgh.

SECTION III.

HOLINESS IN THE LATER BOOKS OF THE OLD TESTAMENT.

THROUGHOUT the entire Old Testament the same meaning is found. The words of Josh. iii, 5, " Sanctify yourselves ; for to-morrow Jehovah will do wonders among you," recall Exod. xix, 10 ; those of Josh. v, 15, " The place whereon thou art standing is holiness," recall Exod. iii, 5. " All the silver and gold . . . is holiness to Jehovah : into the treasury of Jehovah it shall come." Josh vi, 19. " They sanctified Kadesh in Galilee to be a city of refuge," xx, 7 ; for these stood in special relation to God. The words of Josh xxiv, 19, " A holy God is he ; a jealous God is he," reminds us of the close connection of the holiness and the jealousy of God. For he who claimed the absolute proprietorship of Israel could tolerate no rival. Micah's mother said, in Judg. xvii, 3, " I have altogether sanctified the silver to Jehovah ; " for she supposed that by using the money to make an image she was devoting it to his service.

In the book of Psalms the word sanctify is never found—a clear proof that it was not equivalent to " purify," an idea which not unfrequently occurs. It is found only once in the other poetical books, in Job. i, 5 ; and then in a ritual sense. In Psa. lxxxix, 5, 7, as in

Job. v, 1 ; xv, 15, the word holy or saint denotes the
angels. And naturally so ; for our chief thought of
them is that they stand in special relation to God and
are doing his work. " Aaron, the holy one of Jehovah,"
Psa. cvi, 16, recalls the ritual phraseology of the law.
Very rarely in the poetical books are good men called
holy ; for example, Psa. xvi, 3, " To the holy ones which
are in the earth ; " Psa. xxxiv. 9, " Fear Jehovah, ye his
holy ones." These passages were prompted by a consciousness that the good man stands in a special relation
to God as God's own, and are thus an approach to the
New Testament use of the word. This use was rare,
because as yet holiness was revealed only in symbolic
outline. The inward reality underlying his symbolic
form could not be clearly seen until the appearance of
him who was a perfect embodiment in flesh and blood
of what the symbols dimly shadowed.

In the later books of the Old Testament traces of this
moral sense are occasionally found. The lady of Shunem
observed that Elisha stood specially near to God, and
spoke of him in 2 Kings iv, 9 as a " man of God, a holy
man." In prophetic vision Isaiah sees the day when
" all that are left in Jerusalem will be called holy," iv, 3 ;
" A people of holiness," lxii, 12. In the book of Daniel,
for example, vii, 18, 22, 25, 27, the word holy is a frequent designation of the future people of God.

It is interesting to observe that in Isa. xiii, 3, the
destroyers of Babylon are called " God's sanctified ones,"
because working out the purposes of God. Similarly,

Jer. li, 27, 28: "Sanctify against her the nations, the kings of the Medes." Notice also Micah iii, 5: "He that putteth not into their mouth they" (the wicked priests) "sanctify war against him." They proclaim war, professing to do so in the service of God. Compare also 2 Kings x. 20: "Sanctify an assembly for Baal," the only passage in which the word is used for devotion to a false god. But it is used by one who for the moment professes to believe that Baal is the true God.

In the book of Psalms the word holy is sometimes, and the word holiness very frequently, applied to God. In the vision recorded in Isa. vi, the seraphim proclaim three times that God is holy. And very frequently throughout the book of Isaiah we meet the phrase, "The Holy One of Israel" (in Isa. xxix, 23, "The Holy One of Jacob"), which by an interesting coincidence is recorded in 2 Kings xix, 22 as spoken by Isaiah. The same phrase is found in Psa. lxxi, 22; lxxviii, 41; lxxxix, 19, and Jer. l, 29. This phrase is in complete accord with the explanation given above of the holiness of God in the books of the law. "The Holy One of Israel" is the exact counterpart to "holiness to Jehovah;" just as in Lev. xx, 24, 26, etc, "I am Jehovah," is practically equivalent to "I, Jehovah, am holy." Jehovah and Israel stood in special relation each to the other. Therefore Jehovah was "The Holy One of Israel" and Israel was "holy to Jehovah." This mutual relation rested upon God's claim that Israel should be specially his; and this claim implied that in a special manner he would be-

long to Israel. This claim was a manifestation of the
nature of God. And it was the first thought about God
which would rise to the mind of the pious Israelite.

The obligation to sanctify Jehovah, already met with
in the books of the law, is also found in Isa. v, 16:
" Jehovah of hosts will be exalted in the judgment, and
the holy God will be sanctified in righteousness." And
in the book of Ezekiel we are frequently told that God
will be sanctified, especially by punishing the wicked.
For the punishment of those who reject him will reveal
the inviolability of God's claim to the allegiance and devotion of men.

In the books of Chronicles and Nehemiah the words
holy and sanctify are frequent, always in a ritual sense.
So in 2 Chron. xxiii, 6: " Let none come into the house
of Jehovah except the priests: they shall come in; for
they are holy."

I will conclude our study of the Old Testament by
quoting the last words of one of the latest and greatest
of the prophets, who foresaw in the far future the realization of the ancient symbols. In Zech. xiv, 20, 21, we
read: " In that day shall there be upon the bells of the
horses, Holiness to Jehovah: and the pots in the house
of Jehovah shall be like the bowls before the altar. And
every pot in Jerusalem and in Judah shall be holiness for Jehovah of hosts. . . . And there shall not be a
Canaanite any more in the house of Jehovah of hosts,
in that day."

The above quotations are samples of the use of a word

found in the Old Testament more than eight hundred
times.   The frequency and variety of its use make the
meaning quite clear and beyond doubt.   In an immense
majority of instances the word holy is spoken of creatures rational or irrational, and denotes that they stand
in a special relation to God as his possession, and that,
therefore, man may not use or touch them except at the
bidding of God and to do his work.   This peculiar relation to God arises from his own claim, in consequence of
which they stand apart from any thing man does or fails
to do, in a new and solemn relation to him.   This may
be called objective holiness.   It is the most common
sense of the word.   In this sense God sanctified these
objects for himself.   But since some of the objects claimed
were intelligent beings, and the others were in the control of such, the word sanctify denotes also their own
formal surrender of themselves and their possessions to
God.   This may be called subjective holiness.   We also
found six cases in the books of the law, and very many
in the psalms and prophets, in which the words holy and
holiness are predicated of or attributed to God; and
from these we learned that God's claim was not merely
occasional, but was an outflow of his essence. ⟨ We saw
that God sanctified himself by vindicating in word or
deed the inviolability of his claim; that men sanctified
God and God's name by rendering to him the devotion
he claims, and that, as the one Being who claims unlimited and absolute ownership and supreme devotion, God
is the holy One.

SECTION IV.

The Word Holy in the Septuagint Version and in the Apocrypha.

WE come now to the translation of the Seventy, in which we see Hebrew thought robing itself in European language, and thus unconsciously equipping itself for the conquest of the West—a conquest destined to exercise so mighty an influence upon the history of the kingdom of God and the fortunes of the world. A word was needed to receive and to carry forth unalloyed to the nations who spoke Greek the great truths wrapped up in the Hebrew word we have just been studying.

A very common word, an almost exact Greek counterpart of the Hebrew word, was ready for the translator's use. Whatever man or thing was supposed to stand in some special relation to a deity was said, without consideration of its inherent quality, to be ἱερός. And we have seen that this was the radical Hebrew conception of holiness. It is, however, significant that the Greek word is never used, whereas the Hebrew often is, as an attribute of God. But in a few passages Greek writers assert the great truth that of all sacred objects the good man is the most sacred, and they thus approach the moral conception of holiness, of which we have found traces in the Old Testament, and which is so conspicuous a feature of the New. Therefore, in spite of the above-mentioned shortcoming, it might seem that the word ἱερός was no unworthy Greek representative of the Hebrew conception of holiness.

From this honor, however, the word was, by the Seventy translators, with one consent utterly and rudely thrust out. As a rendering of the adjective "holy" it never occurs. And only once is the substantive ἱερόν used in its frequent New Testament sense of "sanctuary;" namely, in that one strange passage (Ezek. xxviii, 18) in which we read of the sanctuary, not of Jehovah, but of Tyre. The reason is not far to seek. Ἱερός had been polluted by contact with the corruptions of idolatry, and was, therefore, unfit for service in the temple of God. Of this we have had an illustration in the "sacred" prostitutes of Corinth. It is true that in the Hebrew language a similar corruption had defiled (see Deut. xxiii, 17) one member of the family of sacred words. But the defiled member was rigidly excluded from the service of God, and the defilement went no further, whereas in Greek the defilement reached and saturated every member. With the Hebrew word, as a result of its consecration to the service of Jehovah and in spite of the occasional profanation of sacred things, were associated ideas of purity and goodness. With the Greek word, in consequence of the fearful debasement of idolatry, were associated conceptions the vilest and worst. Another word must, therefore, be found to carry to the nations of the West, in its purity, the Hebrew conception of holiness.

This honorable office was conferred on the comparatively rare word ἅγιος. Its rarity was a recommendation. For that it had so few associations of its own made it the fitter to take up the meaning and appropriate to itself the associations of the Hebrew word. And its associations, though few, were suitable. In classic Greek it is never found as a predicate of gods or men, and was, therefore, free from the ideas of imperfection and sin which belonged in the minds of idolaters both to gods and men. It is frequently used by Herodotus and occasionally by other writers to describe temples of special sacredness, and seems to denote the reverence which their connection with the deity, ἱερόν, gave them a right to claim. It is probably akin to ἅζομαι, used by Homer (*Iliad.* i, 21, etc.) to denote reverence for the gods and for parents. It was evidently a nobler and purer word than ἱερός. The difference arose from the fact that, owing to the degradation of idolatry, there were objects supposed to stand in close relation to the gods which had no claim whatever to man's real reverence. A very good instance of the distinction is quoted in Cremer's valuable *New Testament Lexicon*, from Plutarch, *Conviv.* 5, 682, C: "Amorous and untamed men are unable to abstain even from the most holy bodies;" which Cremer properly contrasts with the "sacred" bodies of the "sacred slaves," Strabo, 6, 272.

Such being the associations of the words, the Seventy translators, moved by a delicate appreciation of the difference between the gods of heathendom and the one God of Israel, rejected ἱερός, which was already occupied by conceptions partly impure, and chose ἅγιος, which was in part unoccupied and in part occupied by a pure conception, namely, reverence, to receive and bear to the nations of Europe the definite Mosaic conception of holiness. To represent the modifications of the Hebrew word the Seventy thrust aside the existing, though rare, derivative of ἅγος, and derived directly from ἅγιος a family of words of which every member was altogether new in Greek literature.

It is worthy of notice that in Judges xvi, 16, for the words Nazarite of God, which the Alexandrian MS. reproduces, the Vatican MS. gives ἅγιος Θεοῦ. And rightly so. For the Nazarite was holy. And this holiness Samson's deep sin could not obliterate.

In the Apocrypha the use of ἅγιος and its cognates corresponds exactly to its use in the Septuagint—that is, to the use of the Hebrew word. The purely ritual use is found in Judith xi, 13: "The first-fruits of the corn, and the tithes of the wine and the oil, which they kept, having sanctified them for the priests who present themselves before the face of our God." So 1 Macc. x, 39: "For the holy things which are at Jerusalem, for the expenses suitable for the holy things." Compare Sir. xlv, 4, " In his faith and meekness he sanctified (Moses), he chose him out of all flesh ;" and v. 6, "he exalted Aaron to be holy like him." In v. 10 we have Aaron's holy robe. So Sir. xlix, 12: "A people holy for the Lord, prepared for glory of eternity." From the days of the week God "exalted and sanctified the Sabbath," Sir. xxxiii, (xxxvi.) 9. God is the holy One from heaven, who redeemeth Judah from the host of Sennacherib: Sir. xlviii, 20. In 2 Macc. viii, 23 we read of the holy book. In 2 Macc. v, 15, the word ἅγιον appears in the sense of sanctuary. This was now safe, for the conception of holiness was now indissolubly linked to ἅγιος.

In the Apocrypha, as in the version of the Seventy, the word ἅγιος simply takes up the ideas associated with the Hebrew word and passes them on unchanged, as an almost lifeless body awaiting the new life soon to be breathed into it by a new and more glorious revelation.

SECTION V.

HOLINESS IN THE NEW TESTAMENT.

THE writers of the New Testament perpetuate and develop the Old Testament conception of holiness. It was still remembered that the first-born was holy to the Lord. Luke ii, 23. The emphatic teaching of Exod. xxix, 37, etc., that "whatever touches the altar" shall be holy, was not forgotten. For Matt. xxiii, 17, 19, Christ appeals in argument to the truth that the temple had already sanctified (aorist) the gold used in its construction, and that the altar day by day sanctified (present tense) the gifts laid upon it. As in the Septuagint version of Neh. xi, 1, so in Matt. iv, 5, xxvii, 53, Jerusalem is called the holy city. For it stood in a special relation to God. The words of Stephen, recorded in Acts vii, 33, prove that the opening words of the Mosaic revelation (Exod. iii, 5) still lived in the memory of the people. The temple was still the holy place, Matt. xxiv, 15; Acts vi, 13; xxi, 28. The word holy used in Job v, 1; xv, 15; Dan. viii, 13, to designate the angels as persons who stand in a special relation to God and do his bidding, is applied to them as an epithet in Matt. xxv. 31; Luke ix, 26; Acts x, 22. Similarly, though in lower degree, as in Jer. i, 5, so in Luke i, 70; Acts iii, 21, it is applied to the prophets. Herod knew (Mark vi, 20) that the Bap-

tist was a man whose conduct agreed with the law, and
who stood in a special relation to God, " a righteous and
holy man."

Very conspicuous, especially in the writings of St.
Luke, is the term Holy Spirit, already used in the Septuagint as a rendering of the phrase " Spirit of Holiness"
in Psa. li, 11 ; Isa. lxiii, 10.　The Spirit of God claims
the epithet as being in a very special manner the source
of an influence of which God is the one and only aim.
All other influences tend away from God.　He is, therefore, in a sense shared by no other inward motive principle, the Holy Spirit.

The holiness of God, so solemnly asserted in Leviticus
and so frequently in Isaiah, is mentioned in the New
Testament only in John xvii, 11 ; Heb. xii, 10 ; 1 Pet. i,
15, 16 (quoted from Lev. xi, 44) ; Rev. iv, 8 (a repetition
of Isa. vi, 3) ; and Rev. vi, 10.　The meaning of the word
holy in these passages is practically the same as that
deduced from its similar use in the Old Testament, except that our conception of the holiness of God increases
with our increasing perception of the greatness of his
claim upon us.　As we bow before God we remember
that he claims from us a lifelong and unlimited service—
claims that all our powers, possessions, and opportunities
be used to advance his purposes even to the disregard of
personal comfort and worldly advantage and life itself,
and that this claim springs from the very essence of God.
This conception of God is one of the most solemn we can
have, and is embodied in the term " the holy God."　The

rarity of this attribute of God in the New Testament is accounted for by the revelation of a still nobler attribute, the love of God. At Sinai God spoke his claim in a voice of thunder. But from the cross of Christ he reveals the love which moves him to claim our devotion, and this greater revelation made the earlier one less conspicuous. Moreover, as we shall see, God's claim to the absolute devotion of his people was embodied in a common designation of Christians.

The meaning of 1 Pet. iii, 15, " Sanctify Christ as Lord in your hearts," (the reading is undoubted) is, render to Christ in the inmost chamber of your being the reverence which belongs to him who claims to be your proprietor and master ; and is little or nothing less than a declaration that Christ is divine. That the name of God may evoke such reverence in the hearts of those who speak or hear it is the meaning of the Lord's Prayer, " Thy name be sanctified."

So far the conception of holiness has advanced little beyond the development attained in the Old Testament. The greater frequency of holiness as an attribute of the Spirit is, however, a mark of that better covenant of which the indwelling and sanctifying presence of the Spirit is so conspicuous and glorious a feature. And the similarity of the use of the word in the Old and the New Testaments is a proof how fully the Old Testament conception of holiness lived on in the minds of the people.

SECTION VI.

The Holiness of Jesus Christ.

IN the person and life of the incarnate Son of God we
see the full development and realization of the biblical idea of holiness.　On the eve of his incarnation
(Luke i, 35) he was announced by the angel as the holy
thing; the neuter form leaving out of sight all except
that he would be an embodiment of holiness.　He was
acknowledged both by his disciples (John vi, 69) and by
evil spirits (Mark i, 24) to be the holy one of God.　Himself declared, as recorded in John x, 36; xvii, 19, that
the Father had sanctified him and sent him into the
world, and that day by day he sanctified himself.　The
ascended Saviour is spoken of in Acts iii, 14; iv, 27, as
the holy and just one, the holy servant of God.　St. Paul
teaches (in Rom. i, 4) that he was marked out as Son of
God according to a spirit of holiness.　He is probably
the holy one of 1 John ii, 20; and in Rev. iii, 7, he is
called holy and true.

　Since holiness is thus solemnly predicated of the Son
of God we expect to find in him a fully-developed im-
personation of the idea imperfectly shadowed forth in
the Mosaic ritual.　We expect to find him standing in a
special relation to God and living a life of which the one
and only aim is to advance the purposes of God.　Our

expectation is fulfilled. The Son of God declared, in John iv, 34, " It is my meat to do the will of him that sent me and to complete his work ; " in chap. v, 19, "The Son cannot do any thing of himself, but what he sees the Father doing ; " in v. 30, " I seek not my own will, but the will of him that sent me ; " in chap. vi, 38, "Because I have come down from heaven not that I may do my own will but the will of him that sent me ; " chap. xvii, 4, " I have glorified thee on the earth, having finished the work which thou gavest me to do." We read in Rom. vi, 10, that " The life which he lives, he lives for God ; " in chap. xv, 3, " Christ did not please himself ; " in 1 Cor. iii, 23, "You are Christ's and Christ is God's ; " in Heb. iii, 2, " Being faithful to him that made him ; " in chap. ix, 14, " He offered himself spotless to God."

In Jesus we see a life, lived in human flesh and blood, of which God was the one and only aim. All the powers, time, and opportunities of Jesus were used, not to gratify self, but to work out the Father's purposes. And this devotion to the Father was rational. The human intelligence of the man Jesus, mysteriously informed by the divine intelligence of the eternal Son of God, comprehended and fully approved and appropriated the Father's eternal purpose to save mankind through the death of his Son ; and of this intelligent approval every word and act of the human life of Jesus was a perfect outworking. And in this sense, in a degree infinitely surpassing whatever had been known before, the incarnate Son of God was holy. Consequently his body was a temple, John ii, 21, and a sacrifice, Heb. x, 10, and himself a high-priest, chap. iii, 1. Whatever holiness belonged to the vessels and ritual of the Mosaic covenant belonged to him and to his life ; whatever in them was imperfect found in him its full realization.

We notice further that, under the old covenant, the holy men were separated by their holiness from the common work of common life. This was very conspicuous in the last of the prophets, in that " righteous and holy man" (Mark vi, 20) in whose person and teaching was summed up whatever had been revealed under the earlier dispensation. The contrast of John and Jesus is the contrast of holiness as revealed in the law and as revealed in the Gospel. John lived in the wilderness, away from the dwellings of men, and ate strange food. Jesus lived a common life, toiling at a trade, enjoying social intercourse, partaking of human hospitality, and eating the food set before him. This teaches plainly that holiness in its highest degree—that is, the highest conceivable devotion to God and to the advancement of his kingdom —does not imply separation from the common business of life. And when we see Jesus using the opportunities afforded him by this common intercourse with men to advance the interests of the kingdom of God we learn that even the common things of daily life may be laid on the altar of God as a means of doing his holy work.

We saw that under the old covenant devotion to God implied separation from whatever, in symbol or reality, was opposed to God. Now all sin is opposed to God ;

for sin, in whatever form or degree, tends to misery and destruction, whereas God's purpose is life and happiness. Consequently the holiness of Jesus involves his absolute separation from all sin.

Again, the only purpose of God which we can conceive as having a practical bearing upon us is God's purpose to save men from sin and death and to set up the eternal kingdom of which Christ will be king and his people citizens. Consequently, to us devotion to God implies devotion to this one purpose. And this one great divine purpose is inseparably linked with our conception of holiness. Therefore, since to realize this purpose God sent his Son into the world, the Saviour spoke appropriately (John x, 36) of himself as " Him whom the Father sanctified and sent into the world." And in reference to his own daily devotion of himself to this enterprise he said (chap. xvii, 19) " I sanctify myself."

Thus, from the great Author and archetype of renewed humanity, we have obtained a complete conception of holiness. We have seen a man, though God yet perfect man, whose life was a constant and perfect realization of one purpose—a purpose to use all his powers, time, and opportunities to advance the kingdom of God ; and we have seen that this purpose was a result of an intelligent comprehension and full approval of the Father's purpose. In virtue of this intelligent, hearty, continued appropriation of the Father's purpose, and in virtue of its realization in all the details of the Saviour's life, he was called the Holy One of God.

SECTION VII.

The Holiness of the Followers of Christ.

WE now come to study the idea of holiness as embodied in redeemed mankind. In so doing we meet at once a conspicuous difference of the use of the word in the Old and in the New Testament; namely, that in the Acts of the Apostles and elsewhere all church-members are indiscriminately called saints, holy persons. This is a complete contrast with 2 Chron. xxiii, 6: "Let none come into the house of Jehovah except the priests. . . . They shall go in: for they are holiness. And all the people shall keep the watch of Jehovah." But it fulfills the prophecy of Daniel, who speaks in chap. vii, 18, 22, 25, 27, of the future people of God as the "people of the saints of the Most High." This is the use of the adjective holy in five out of every six places in the New Testament in which it is spoken of Christian believers. And its frequency claims for it the first place in our study of the holiness of the followers of Christ. We also notice that the writers of the New Testament call believers saints without thought of the degree of their Christian life or the worthiness of their conduct.

This New Testament use may be explained by an Old Testament analogy. The priests were holy, whatever might be their conduct. Samson was a holy man of God, even in the embrace of Delilah. For God's claim that they should be his had placed them in a new position, and could not be set aside by, although it greatly aggravated the guilt of, their unfaithfulness. Just so God claims for himself all those whom he rescues from the penalty of their sins, and, whatever they may do, his claim puts them in a new and very solemn position. They may be, like the Corinthians (1 Cor. iii, 3), babes in Christ and carnal: like the Corinthians (chap. i, 2), they are still "sanctified in Christ Jesus." The word saint is therefore very appropriate as a designation of the followers of Christ; for it declares what God requires them to be. To admit sin or selfishness into their hearts is sacrilege. Nay, more. It also points out their privilege. By calling his people saints God declares his will that we live a life of which he is the one and only aim. Therefore, since our own efforts have proved that such a life is utterly beyond our power, we may take back to God the name he gives us and claim that it be realized by his power in our heart and life. To keep these all-important truths ever before the mind of believers the Holy Spirit moved the early Christians to speak of themselves as saints, as holy men. This is the objective holiness of the Church of Christ.

But, although, as claimed by God, all the children of God are holy, it is evident that the full idea of holiness is realized in them only so far as they yield to God the devotion he claims. To bear the name of saint and yet be animated, in part, by a worldly spirit, is evidently a contradiction in terms. Consequently, in a few passages, the word holy denotes actual and absolute devotion to God. And holiness is set before the people of God as a standard for their attainment. So 1 Cor. vii, 34, "That she may be holy both in body and spirit;" parallel with, "How she may please the Lord." Eph. i, 4, "That we may be holy and blameless;" chap. v. 27; Col. i, 22: 1 Thess. v, 23, "May the God of peace sanctify you;" Heb. xii, 14, "Follow after holiness;" 1 Pet. i, 15, "Be yourselves holy in all behavior." In these passages the word holy denotes a realization in man of God's purpose that he live a life of which God is the one and only aim. In other words, that man is holy who looks upon himself and all his possessions as belonging to God, and uses all his time, powers, and opportunities, to work out the purposes of God—that is, to advance the kingdom of Christ. This is the subjective holiness to which God calls his people.

We also notice that frequently in the New Testament the ideal life which Christ died to realize in his people is said to be a life in which all our powers are put forth to advance the purposes of God. So Rom. vi, 11, "Reckon yourselves to be living for God in Christ Jesus." Ver. 19, "Present the members of your body, as servants, to righteousness, for sanctification." Chap. xiv, 7, "None of us lives for himself: for, if we live, we live for the Lord." 2 Cor. v, 15, "He died that they who live may live no longer for themselves but for him who on their behalf died and rose."   1 Cor. vi, 19; iii, 23, "Ye are not your own, but Christ's."   The life here described is a life of holiness.

Since holiness is God's claim to the service of his creatures the word is predicated of both spirit and body: 1 Cor. vii, 34; Rom. xii, 1; 1 Thess. v, 23.   For God claims even our body, that its powers may work out his purposes.

Since holiness, as set forth in the Mosaic ritual, was a prophetic outline of the holiness required in us, the various holy objects of that ritual were types, as of Christ; so also of his followers.   We are a temple, 1 Cor. iii, 16; vi, 19; a priesthood, 1 Pet. ii, 5. 9; a sacrifice, Rom. xii, 1.   Our future life will be a Sabbath-keeping, Heb. iv, 9.   We also notice that in the New Testament the word sanctify occurs most frequently in that portion of it which deals most fully with the Mosaic ritual: the Epistle to the Hebrews.   This suggests that in the apostolic Church the word had not shaken off, as to a large extent it has now, its original connection with that ritual.   To this original reference of the word we must ever recur if we wish to think of holiness as it was understood by the early Christians.

Very interesting is 1 Cor. vii, 14: "The unbelieving husband is sanctified in the wife." *   Since the people of God are holy it might be thought that, as taught in Ezra ix, 2, the seed of holiness ought to separate itself from contact with the unholy.   St. Paul says, No.   The

---

* This passage I have expounded at full in *The Expositor* for November, 1879.

Christian wife, in virtue of the universal priesthood of believers, lays her husband upon the altar of God, and in all her treatment of him seeks to advance the purposes of God. Therefore, in the subjective world of the wife's inner life, the husband, unbeliever though he be, is a holy object, and the wife's intercourse with him is a service of God. St. Paul proves the correctness of this view by showing that if the principle of separation from the unbelieving were accepted it would in some cases compel the Christian mother to forsake her children, who evidently, in spite even of their possible rejection of Christianity, had a claim upon their mother's care. Whereas, he says, on the principle that to the Christian wife the heathen husband is a sacred object, the children also are sacred, and therefore fit objects of a Christian mother's care. And if it be right for her to live with her children, some of whom may be adult idolaters, on the same principle it is right for her to live with her husband. Thus, from the case of the children, St. Paul proves the case of the husband.

Equally interesting is 1 Tim. iv, 4: "Every creature of God is good, and nothing is to be cast away, when received with thanksgiving: for it is sanctified through the word of God and prayer." The word of God is the voice of God (Gen. i, 29; ix, 3), by which God devoted vegetables and animals to be food for his rational creatures. This universal word was for a time restricted by the law, which declared that only certain specified animals were holy; but the restriction had been solemnly revoked (Acts x, 13) and the original word was again in force. Thus, by the word of God, all manner of food was consecrated for the use of the sacred people. The general word prayer includes the thanksgiving of ver. 4. Our thanks to God is the testimony of our conscience that we believe our food to be his gift to us, and is, therefore, a proof that we eat it for the Lord. " He eats for the Lord : for he gives thanks to God." Rom. xiv, 6. Consequently, whatever food we eat with genuine thanksgiving is, by God's original word, and by our thanks, which is a recognition of that original word, made holy food, suitable for the holy people. But the same food, if eaten without this intelligent recognition of it as God's gift, would, in spite of its objective sanctification by God's original word, be unholy and defiling. Rom. xiv, 14.

We have now, by study of the Old and New Testaments, obtained a clear conception of holiness as understood by the writers of the Bible. It is God's claim that his creatures use all their powers and opportunities to work out his purposes. We have seen that holiness, thus understood, is an attribute of God. For his claim springs from his nature, even from that love which is the very essence of God. His love to us moves him to claim our devotion : for only by absolute devotion to him can we attain our highest happiness. We have also seen the idea of holiness realized in the Son of God, who took upon him our flesh, lived a human life on earth, and now lives a glorified human life upon the throne of God, simply and only to accomplish the Father's purposes. We have the same idea realized in the Spirit of God, who ever goes forth from the Father that he may lead us to the Father, and whose every influence tends to accomplish the Father's purposes. The same idea is in part realized in all the adopted children of God. For God has claimed them to be his own, and his claim puts them, whatever they may do, in a new and solemn position. But the complete idea of holiness is realized in them only so far as their entire activity of body and mind are the outworking of a single purpose to accomplish the purposes of God.

It has been well said that purpose is the autograph of mind. Wherever purpose is there is mind. And wherever mind is directed toward the great source of mind there is holiness.

SECTION VIII.

CHRISTIAN HOLINESS IS THE TRUE EXPLANATION OF THE MOSAIC RITUAL.

HITHERTO we have sought by study of the Mosaic ritual to understand the holiness which Christ came to realize in his people. This process may be profitably reversed. The holiness proclaimed by Christ explained, and is the only conceivable explanation of, a great part of the Mosaic ritual. It has frequently been observed that the only explanation of the Mosaic sacrifices, and of the prominence given to blood in the Mosaic ritual, is the great truth that in later ages Christ came to save mankind by his own death, and that apart from the death of Christ the Old Testament sacrifices are meaningless and therefore unaccountable. It is equally true that the prominence given in the old covenant to ceremonial holiness receives its only explanation from the holiness taught by Christ. For from the New Testament point of view we see that in order to teach men, in the only way they could understand, that God claims that they look upon themselves as belonging to him, and use all their powers and time to work out his purposes—we see that in order to teach men this God set apart for himself, in outward and visible and symbolic form, a certain place and certain men, things, and periods of time.　Afterward, when in this way men had become familiar with the idea of holiness, God proclaimed in Christ that this idea must be realized in every man and place and thing and time.　Thus in the biblical conception of holiness we have an explanation of a marked and otherwise inexplicable feature of the old covenant; we have a link binding the covenants together, and a light which each covenant reflects back on the other.

SECTION IX.

HOLINESS AS OPPOSED TO SIN.

SO far we have studied the biblical conception of holiness without any direct reference to sin. Indeed, we have found the word holy predicated of not a few objects in reference to which there could be no thought of sin or of the absence of sin—for example, the gold of the temple. But it is quite clear that, when predicated of men, holiness—that is, devotion to God, implies complete victory over all sin. For all sin, in thought, word or deed, tends to frustrate God's purposes. And as soon as we resolve to live for God, devoting to his service all we have and are, and in proportion to the earnestness of our resolve, we become conscious of a force within us tending to hinder, and actually hindering, our earnest purpose. This adverse force is in part a result of Adam's sin, and in part of our own indulgence of personal sin. It is directly opposed to God and to his purposes. Therefore there can be no complete devotion to God without complete victory over this inward force of evil.

We notice also that in Scripture deliverance from sin is frequently mentioned as a necessary antecedent of that devotion to himself which God requires. In John xvii, 15, 16, the Saviour, praying for his disciples, asked first, " Keep them from the evil ; " then " sanctify them in the truth." So 1 Cor. vi, 11, "You have been washed, you have been sanctified;" 2 Cor. vii, 1, "Let us cleanse ourselves (aorist) from all defilement of flesh and spirit, accomplishing holiness;" Rom. vi, 11, "Reckon yourselves to be dead to·sin, but living for God;" Eph. v, 26, 27, "That he might sanctify it, having cleansed it by the laver of the water in the word, that he might himself present to himself the Church glorious, not having spot or wrinkle, or any such thing, but that it may be holy and blameless." In this last passage holy and blameless correspond respectively to present to himself and not having spot. In Rom. vi, 11, dead to sin denotes, in the strongest possible manner, complete separation through the death of Christ from all sin.

On the relation of holiness to sin 1 Thess. iv, 3 casts light. The words "your sanctification" are in apposition with "will of God;" and "this" points to "that you abstain from fornication, that each one," etc. God's will about us—that is, his sanctification of us, claiming our devotion, involves our abstinence from whatever we know to be opposed to him. And in giving us the gospel call (ver. 7) God was sanctifying us for himself. To this passage we have in Lev. xi, 43, 44, an Old Testament parallel.

It is, however, worthy of notice that, although frequently mentioned in close connection with deliverance from sin, holiness is never a synonym of purity. We never find the exact phrase "sanctify from sin." Even in the comparison of Heb. ix, 13, 14, the word sanctify is replaced in the second member by cleanse. And the reason is not far to seek. Although without purity we cannot be subjectively holy, yet holiness is much more than purity. For purity is a mere negative excellence, and might be conceived of as existing without activity. Indeed, a mere negative sinlessness has sometimes been the aim of mistaken spiritual effort. But holiness implies the most intense mental and bodily activity of which we are capable. For it is the employment of all our powers and opportunities to advance God's purposes; and this implies the use of our intelligence to learn how best to do his work and the bodily effort which his work requires. And in order to keep before us the essentially positive nature of holiness the word is never used to denote simple victory over sin.

Notice also that just as there cannot be holiness without purity so, practically, there cannot be purity without holiness. We shall never be set free from sin until all our powers are devoted to God. For sin arises from the erection of self into the supreme power within us. And self will reign until a mightier one occupy the throne it has usurped.

SECTION X.

How we Become Holy.

THE teaching of the foregoing section prompts at once the question, How may we become holy? How may we, in spite of the inborn corruption of our nature, strengthened by the accumulated force of our own past sins—how may we live a life of which God shall be the one and only aim?

The prayers of Christ (John xvii, 17) and of St. Paul (1 Thess. v, 23) teach plainly that our sanctification is a work of God. And these prayers refer, not to the objective holiness which claims us for God, but to the subjective holiness in which the claimed devotion is actually rendered. For both prayers were offered on behalf of those who were already objectively holy. And the words of Heb. xii, 10, "That we may partake his holiness," imply that our holiness is an outflow of God's holiness. We expect, therefore, to find that the devotion to God of ourselves, our powers, and our possessions, is a result not only of God's original claim, but of his power working in us the devotion he requires.

The objective sanctification of the Corinthian Christians is said in 1 Cor. i, 2, to be in Christ. In Heb. ii, 11, Christ is called "the sanctifier," and is said in 1 Cor. 1, 30, to have become to us sanctification. And in Heb. x, 10,

14, 29; xiii, 12, we are taught that the sacrificial offering of Christ and the shedding of his blood are the means of our sanctification. "He died that he might be our Lord," Rom. xiv, 9; and "that we may live for him," 2 Cor. v, 15. We learn, then, that our holiness comes through Christ's death. This is explained in Rom. iii, 26, where we are taught that God gave his Son to die to make it consistent with his righteousness to justify those whom his own law had condemned to die. For God cannot sanctify the unforgiven.

If therefore to-day, in response to God's claim, we are living for God, it is because centuries ago the Holy One of God consecrated with his own blood the altar on which are laid to-day in willing sacrifice whatever we have and are. And in the same sense we say, in the words of 1 John i, 7, "The blood of Jesus, his Son, cleanses us from all sin."

But the relation between our holiness and Christ is more intimate even than this. The words of John xvii, 19, "On their behalf I sanctify myself that they also themselves may be sanctified," teach plainly that our holiness is an outflow of his. The Son devoted himself without reserve to the Father's great purpose of saving men that his followers might be animated by a like devotion. The change from the active to the passive voice of the verb marks the difference between the Sanctifier and the sanctified. St. Paul, in Rom. vi, 11, after teaching that Christ is dead to sin and living for God, bids us claim a similar death and life. And in Gal. ii, 20, after stating the purpose for which he had died to the law, namely, that he may live for God, he says, " No longer do I live, but in me Christ lives." In other words, our devotion to God is a result of inward spiritual contact with him who once lived a human life on earth and now lives a glorified human life upon the throne of God simply and only to work out the Father's purposes. We live for God because Christ does so, and because Christ lives in us and we in him.

In 2 Thess. ii, 13, and 1 Pet. i, 2, we read of sanctification of the Spirit; and in Rom. xv, 16, St. Paul expresses a desire that the Gentiles, offered in sacrifice to God, may be sanctified in the Holy Spirit. This we understand. For the Spirit of Christ is the agent of the spiritual contact with Christ which imparts to us his presence and reproduces in us his life. As we have seen, every impulse of the spirit is toward God; and he is given to us that he may fill our hearts, may become the soul of our soul and lead out toward God our thoughts, purposes, words, and actions. And he is bearer of the power as well as of the holiness of Christ. By his omnipotence the Spirit of God rolls back and completely neutralizes the evil forces within us, so that they no longer defile us, and in spite of them bears upward our entire being in absolute devotion to God. Now both the Son and the Spirit are the Father's gift to us, and they were given in order to rescue us from a life devoted to self and to work in us devotion to God. Therefore the entire redemptive economy is an offspring of the holi-

ness as well as of the love of God.   And our holiness is
entirely God's work in us, a realization of his eternal
purpose, and a satisfaction of a claim which has its root
in the nature of God.   In this sense we partake his
holiness.

The word of God is the means of our purity, John
xv, 3, and of our sanctification, chap. xvii, 17. If to-day
we are victorious over sin and are living for God it is
because we have heard the word and the truth of God.

In 2 Thess. ii, 13, sanctification of the spirit is placed
in close connection with belief of the truth.   And from
Acts xxvi, 18, we learn that not only forgiveness of sins,
but a lot among the sanctified, is obtained by faith in
Christ.   This accords with the broad principles asserted
in Mark ix, 23, " All things are possible to him who be-
lieves ; " in Eph. ii, 8, " You have been saved through
faith ; " in Gal. iii, 14, " That we may receive the promise
of the Spirit through faith ; " and in Acts xv, 9, " By faith
having purified their hearts ; " and with a great mass of
Bible teaching, which I have not space here to quote and
expound.   One passage, however, claims special attention.   In Rom. vi, 11, St. Paul bids us to " Reckon ourselves to be dead to sin, but living for God in Christ
Jesus."   This reckoning is the mental process of faith,
for it results in assurance resting upon the promise of
God. Now we cannot do wrong in obeying the apostle—
that is, in reckoning ourselves to be dead to sin and
henceforth living for God.   But up to this moment we
have been sadly alive to sin and living in part to please

ourselves. Our own past experience contradicts flatly the reckoning which St. Paul bids us make. But as we stand beneath the cross of Him who died that we might live no longer for ourselves but for him, and as we feel the constraining power of his mysterious love, we dare not hesitate. And with a confidence that seems to us akin to madness, but which is commanded by God, we venture to believe, at the apostle's bidding, that we are now dead to sin, and that from this moment we shall live for God, and that in this separation from sin and devotion to God we shall be maintained to the end of life by the presence and power of the Holy Spirit. And, while we thus believe, the command of God, which in believing we obey, is itself a pledge that in the moment of our faith God works in us that which he bids us believe. Else the reckoning which at his bidding we make is false and his word a deception. Therefore, just as we obtain forgiveness by believing that in the moment of our faith and through the death of Christ our sins are forgiven, so, by believing that it is ours, we also so obtain and retain the holiness which God requires and gives.

That God claims from his people unreserved devotion to himself, and that what he claims he works in all who believe it by his own power operating through the inward presence of the Holy Spirit, placing us in spiritual contact with Christ, is the great doctrine of sanctification by faith, than which none is more important. It implies, and is implied in, the twin doctrine of justification by

faith. For the Spirit of holiness given to those who believe is himself a witness of their forgiveness, and that
he is given to rebels to work in them whole-hearted
allegiance reconciles their forgiveness with the holines;
of God. {Moreover, this doctrine implies that complete
victory over sin and full devotion to God are the present
privilege of all believers.} For, if these blessings came
through efforts of our own, they would be obtained only
by gradual and slow approach. But if they are God's
gift to us they may be ours to-day. For we are sure that
God requires them to-day, and what he requires he is
able and willing and is pledged to impart. Although not
stated so formally and conspicuously as justification by
faith, the doctrine of sanctification by faith rests on a
broad and deep foundation of scripture teaching. And
it has been understood by the best men of all Churches
and all ages, and has been the secret of their power.

The faith described above is impossible without self-
consecration. For we cannot believe that God will work
in us a life of which he is the one aim unless we deliberately choose such a life. Therefore the holiness which
comes through spiritual contact with Christ, wrought in
us by the presence and activity of the Holy Spirit, is
obtained by self-consecration and faith. This is clearly
set forth in Rom. vi, 13, where, after bidding us (v. 11)
reckon ourselves to be living for God, St. Paul bids us
present to God ourselves and the members of our bodies.
And in v. 19 we are expressly bidden thus to present
ourselves with a view to sanctification. In accordance

with this, in chap. xii, 1, St. Paul enters upon the subject of Christian morals by bidding us present our bodies to God as a holy sacrifice. We present our bodies to God when we deliberately and solemnly resolve that henceforth our lips shall speak only his message, our hands do his work, our feet run only on his errands, and our life show forth his glory. For from that moment we look upon our bodily powers as belonging no longer to us but to God. And since our body is the only link which unites us to the world in which we live, to present our bodies is to present ourselves. This is self-consecration. To be effective it must be accompanied by sanctifying faith— that is, by an assurance resting upon the word of God, that in spite of the allurements and threats of the world he will maintain in us this resolve and enable us to work it out practically in the details of life. Without this faith our resolve will be in vain. Self-consecration is obedience to God's command claiming from us unreserved devotion ; sanctifying faith is acceptance of the promise that what he claims he will work in us. This claim and this promise are the law and the gospel of holiness.

SECTION XI.

GROWTH IN HOLINESS.

IT is worthy of notice that in the New Testament we never read expressly and unmistakably of sanctification as a gradual process, or, except, perhaps, Rev. xxii, 11, of degrees and growth in holiness.

A gradual process is not necessarily implied in the present participles of Heb. ii, 11 ; x, 14, although it may be suggested by comparison with the participle σωζόμενοι in Luke xiii, 23 ; Acts ii, 47 ; 1 Cor. i, 18 ; 2 Cor. ii, 15. But salvation is expressly said in Rom. v. 9, 10, to await completion in the future even for the justified, and this is never said of sanctification. Moreover the present participle in Rom. iii, 24, referring to those who from time to time are justified, proves that in these two passages the participle may denote those who from time to time are laid on the altar of consecration. And this is supported by the fact that, in contrast to 1 Cor. i, 18, these passages are general assertions in the third person ; whereas in Heb. x, 10, where we read of definite individuals in the first person, we have the perfect tense. Similarly, in Heb. x, 29, we read that the fallen one was once sanctified. Only in Heb. ii, 11 ; x, 14, is the present tense of the word sanctify used of Christian believers. Even in the prayers of John xvii, 17 and 1 Thess. v, 23, and in the purpose of Eph. v, 26 we have the aorist.

The reason of this is not far to seek. The very idea of holiness involves the idea of entirety. For God claims the whole of all we have and are. He claims every moment of our time, every penny we possess, and to be himself the one aim of our every purpose and effort. And he claims all this now; not by gradual, but by immediate surrender. And what he claims he is ready this moment to impart. To keep these great truths clearly before us the sacred writers were held back from speaking of partial or imperfect holiness. So we read without any note of degree: " That she may be holy in body and spirit," 1 Cor. vii, 34; " That it may be holy and spotless," Eph. v. 27; " To present you holy and spotless and unimpeachable," Col. i, 22; " Holy in all behavior," 1 Pet. i, 15. In all these passages the simple word holy denotes absolute devotion to God. And I think that this use of the word corresponds with the experience of the people of God. When we learn that God claims us to be his own, and when, after fruitless personal efforts to render him the devotion he requires, we learn for the first time that God will work in us by the agency of his Spirit and by actual spiritual contact with Christ the devotion he requires, and when we venture to believe that God does now and will henceforth work in us this devotion to himself, and when we find by happy experience that according to our faith it is done to us, the experience thus gained becomes an era in our spiritual life. We feel that we are then holy in a sense unknown to us before.

But there is, nevertheless, a sense in which we may say correctly that holiness is capable of infinite growth. For our devotion to God is still, in a sense, imperfect. At the end of every day we acknowledge that we have failed to work out fully into all the details of the day the one purpose which has by the grace of God been the main-

spring of our action, and that we have often chosen un-
suitable means. But each day we learn better what will
and what will not advance the purposes of God, and each
day our one great purpose permeates more fully our entire thoughts and more fully directs our entire activity.
Moreover, each day brings to us fresh proofs of the faith-
fulness, power, and love of God, and thus increases the
strength of the faith with which we lay hold of all the
benefits promised in his word. Our daily submission to
the guidance of the Spirit brings us more completely
under his holy influence. And since our entire Christian
life takes the form of devotion to God all spiritual progress may be spoken of as growth in holiness.

Moreover it frequently, perhaps usually, happens, in
the case of sanctification, as of justification, that only
gradually we lay hold by faith of the promises of the
Gospel, and therefore obtain by gradual approach these
great benefits. But neither for justification nor for
sanctification is lapse of time needful. God is waiting
to forgive now those who turn from sin and believe his
promise of forgivevess. He claims now from all the
justified unreserved devotion, and what he claims he is
ready to bestow. We have no need to climb to heaven
or descend to the abyss. This has already been done in
Christ. We venture to believe, and the promised blessings are ours.

In 1 Thess. v, 23, the adjective ὁλοτελεῖς denotes, not the measure
or manner, but either the objects or the result of sanctification ;
probably the result, as suggested by the latter part of the word, which

is akin to τέλειος. St. Paul prays that God may sanctify them and thus bring to maturity every part of their being. For this use of the accusative after a verb compare chap. iii, 13, 1 Cor. i, 8 ; Phil. iii, 21. He then prays that their spirit and soul and body—that is, their entire being, may be kept so that no part will be defective, in a manner which will leave no part open to blame in the day of Christ. This verse is interesting as linking together sanctification and Christian maturity. This last word is, I think, a better rendering than perfection, which is generally used in the Authorized Version, but which does not bring out the idea of full growth as contrasted with childhood, as in 1 Cor. xiv, 20 ; Eph. iv, 13 ; Heb. v, 14, and has the great disadvantage of being liable to be misunderstood unless very carefully guarded and explained. From this passage we learn that by working in us devotion to himself God develops to maturity every part of our being.

Very difficult is Rev. xxii, 11, which I read and render, "He that is righteous, let him do righteousness still ; and he that is holy, let him be sanctified still further." As in Matt. xviii, 16, xxvi, 65, ἔτι denotes continuance forward in time or degree. I can only understand these words to exhort the holy man to a further consecration to still higher service. If so, we have here one express mention of growth in holiness.

SECTION XII.

THE EXCELLENCE OF HOLINESS.

THE life revealed to us by our study of the biblical conception of holiness is the ideal Christian life. And it is the noblest ideal we can conceive. For holiness sets before us an aim; the best possible aim; an aim which we can pursue at all times, amid all the various and varying circumstances of life, and in the pursuit of which we can use all our powers. Now, all human effort receives its worth from the object aimed at. No act is trifling which tends to realize some great purpose; whereas the greatest effort which aims at nothing beyond itself is valueless. An aimless life is poor and worthless. But all self-chosen aims must needs be earthly and selfish; for the stream cannot rise above its source. Therefore God, in order to ennoble even the humblest of his children, has given himself and his own purpose of mercy to be their single aim, that they may thus, by directing their efforts toward the realization of his purposes, themselves rise daily toward God.

Again, holiness is a source of every kind of human excellence. For it sets to work all our powers, and sets them to work in the best possible direction. It gives to intellectual effort its noblest aim, namely, to comprehend and to convey to others the life-giving truth of God, and it guards intellectual success from the perils which surround it. It gives the noblest motive for the care and development of the body; for it shows us that the powers even of our perishing body may work out eternal results. And it gives the only pure motive, and a very strong motive, for effort after material good ; for it teaches that this world's wealth may be a means of laying up treasure in heaven. Thus holiness quickens, develops, and elevates all our powers.

Again, holiness not only develops, but satisfies, the intelligence. The mind of the holy man contemplates with full approval the one aim toward which his ceaseless efforts are directed. And his best judgment selects from the means at his disposal those which seem to him most fitted to attain this end. Thus the holy man, and he only, lives a life strictly in accordance with the dictates of his reason. In him that which is by nature highest, namely, the mind, actually rules; and that which is by nature lower, the body, attains its highest well-being by acting under the direction of that which is nobler than itself. Consequently, in him there is perfect harmony and perfect peace, combined with the highest activity.

Again, while we aim at the realization of God's purposes his purposes become our own. That which God desires commends itself to us as worthy of our desire. But God's purpose is the salvation and well-being of mankind. This becomes, therefore, the one purpose of the holy man. But he cherishes this purpose not merely from sympathy with those who are perishing—for some of them have few claims on his sympathy—but because, by devotion to God, he has felt the power of that love which moved the Father to give his only Son to save a ruined world.

We observe that this ideal life is practicable, in the highest degree, to all persons in all positions in life. The man who has fewest powers may use them all for God, and the man whose circumstances are most adverse may yet make it his single aim to do all he can to accomplish the purposes of God; and, if so, even adversity will show forth the glory, and thus help forward the work of him whose grace is ever sufficient. That holiness is possible to all men, always, is some proof that the teaching which claims it is from God.

Another proof of the same is found in the fact that holiness is not only possible in, but fits a man for, every position in life. By making men right with God it makes them right with each other. We have seen that the man who accepts as his own the purposes of God will seek to do all possible good to all within his reach. He will therefore be a good father, a good citizen, a good neighbor, and a tradesman pleasant to deal with.

Lastly, holiness makes us completely free from bondage to the world around and from fear of the uncertainties and perils of life. For the world is in the hand of God, and all its forces are controlled and guided by his power to work out his deliberate purpose. And, if we are holy, his purpose is our purpose. Therefore, strange as the words may seem, between us and every thing around us there is perfect harmony. For whatever comes to us comes from God to help us to accomplish our one earnest purpose. Even the dark things of life are helpers affording us opportunities and aid to serve God. Thus the world is beneath our feet; for it is beneath the feet of him who has made us partners of his throne. And in perfect security and peace, a peace passing understanding, we reign with him.

We can now answer the frequent question, What is religion? It is holiness. That man is most religious who most constantly and intelligently uses his various powers, and the opportunities which each day brings, to work out God's purpose of mercy to mankind. This is the end to which all the so-called means of grace are subordinate. They are of value only so far as they attain this end in us. And we have seen that religion thus understood includes every kind of human excellence and the highest human happiness.

APPENDIX.

T HE purpose of this book is simply to reproduce the conception of holiness as understood by the sacred writers—that is, to determine the sense in which they used the word holy ; not to trace this conception to the eternal reality underlying it, nor to develop its various bearings upon the Christian life. Two matters, however, one in each of these directions, deserve immediate attention.

THE HOLINESS OF GOD.

The declaration at Sinai, "I Jehovah am holy" (Lev. xx, 26), would teach the Israelites that behind and above the holy things and men and times, and yet in closest connection with them, was a holy person—that is, that the separation of these from common use and from man's control had its source in God and in a definite element of his eternal nature. For not otherwise can we explain the use of the common and significant word holy as a predicate of God. We must therefore seek for an element in the nature of God which would prompt him to claim for himself the various holy objects of the old covenant, and to claim in Christ to be the one aim of the entire life and thought and being of his people. And such an element of the divine nature we find every-where in the Bible. As Creator of whatever exists God ever claims to be the sole possessor of all things and the one aim of the entire activity of all his intelligent creatures. That "all things are for him" (Rom. xi, 36) is as absolute a truth as that "all things are from him." For, just as creation is no mere event in the existence of God, but a necessary outflow of his inmost nature, so is his claim to his creatures' absolute devotion. In this sense, then, the word holy is appropriately used as an attribute of God.

This exposition of the term holiness of God has the advantage of retaining the very definite and important idea ever present when the word holy is predicated of men and things, and gives to this term, when predicated of God, a significance quite distinct from that of every other word so predicated. Thus understood the term embodies an indisputable and all-important and very solemn element in the nature of God, one not embodied in any other attribute given to him in the Bible.

The various loose and indefinite meanings attached to the term by most English writers are unworthy of mention—for nearly all of them ignore completely the definite idea every-where embodied in the word holy—and are assumed without any attempt at proof, and apparently without any consciousness of the difficulty of the subject.

The exposition in favor now with German writers is that the word holy is derived from a word denoting separation, and that God is called holy because separate from sin. But this explanation imports into the word holy an entirely new idea, namely, that of sin, and one in no way connected with its supposed original idea, namely, separation. This imported idea cannot be accepted without explanation or proof. If the above derivation be correct, which I am not prepared to deny, the simplest explanation of the common use of the word holy is that it denotes something separated from me—that is, from men generally ; an idea nearly always associated with the word. For all conceptions are looked upon in their relation to ourselves. The use of the word as a predicate of God, which until later days was very rare, is most easily explained, not from its etymology, which in common words like this always retires into the background, but from its very common and definite use in the every-day life of Israel. He was called the holy God because he revealed himself as the God of the Sabbath, the sanctuary, the priesthood, and the sacrifices.

CHRISTIAN PURITY.

In what sense and to what extent will God in this life and now save us from sin ?

"The blood of Jesus cleanses us from all sin," 1 John i, 7. This implies the present removal of whatever makes us spiritually unclean. Of such uncleanness our sense of shame is, I venture to believe, a reliable test and measure. Consequently it is our happy lot to be saved now from whatever pollutes, or, if known to others, would disgrace us.

The original source of personal sin is an inborn tendency to sin, a tendency attested by universal experience. And this tendency to evil has been immensely strengthened by each self-surrender to it— that is, by each act of sin. With this accumulated force of evil we have now to contend. And, from its tremendous and deadly power, the scripture quoted above proclaims that, by the death of Christ, we may now be made free.

This deliverance does not imply the annihilation of the inward tendency to sin, so that we shall no longer find it in us as a force against which we have to watch and to contend. For, if Christ by his own presence and power in our hearts gives us complete and constant victory over the hostile force within us, so that it no longer consciously molds our acts or words or thoughts, we are already saved from all polluting power of sin. A tendency to evil which is every moment trodden underfoot will cause us no spiritual shame. Such victory the words of 1 John i, 7 certainly announce, and, I think, nothing more. Then "will the peace of God guard our thoughts" (Phil. iv, 7) so that they go not astray. Then are we (1 Pet. i, 5) "guarded in the power of God through faith," and (Rom. vi, 11) "dead to sin;" for evil cannot obtain our consent and thus soil our conscience, even though it come with the accumulated force of habit; and through the death of Christ our old life of sin has altogether ceased.

This complete and abiding victory over all sin in thought, word, or deed marks, I venture to believe, a stage of the Christian life higher than justification and sufficiently definite to be an object of thought and faith. The discovery that by faith Jesus saves us now by his power from all sin has been an era in the spiritual life of thousands. It may be suitably called full salvation, or, as we look at its positive side, entire sanctification. But, although day by day as we trample them under foot the inward forces of evil become weaker and by their increasing weakness reveal our spiritual growth, yet I do not find anywhere in the Bible reason to believe that they may now by our faith or at any future time in our lives be entirely annihilated.

The above exposition may be illustrated by a far-reaching analogy found in the solar system. The motive-force in a planet at any moment, which force is an accumulation of its previous motion, would, if the attractive force of the sun were withdrawn, carry the planet from its orbit and to ruin. Whereas, if the inherent force were removed the planet would fall into the sun, thus losing its individual existence. But under the combined influence of these two forces, each exerting its full influence every moment, the planet moves on its appointed path, preserving its individuality yet subordinate to a body immensely greater than itself. So we move in absolute devotion to him from whom we receive light and life and all things.

Similarly we carry in our bodies chemical forces which would destroy us were they not neutralized by the presence of animal life. Yet, in spite of these forces, the body may be in perfect health. For the neutralizing power is sufficient to preserve us. Just so the presence of Christ in our hearts holds back our inborn tendencies to evil, aggravated as they are by personal sin, and preserves us from all corruption. Thus does he save his people from their sins.

In more ways than one Christian purity admits of infinite growth; and for more reasons than one it admits of no finality. Not only do we experience a progressive weakening of the evil forces within us, but even the confidence with which we grasp the promise of purity and obtain its fulfillment dawns in most cases gradually and may increase without limit. And increasing faith is accompanied by victory more and more complete. Moreover, our deliverance from sin is in proportion to our consciousness of sin, and therefore in proportion to the clearness of our spiritual light and our nearness to the light of men. Consequently as day by day we rise nearer to Christ we discover in ourselves subtle elements of sin unsuspected before. And we find by glorious experience that each newly-discovered stain the blood of Jesus washes away. In these senses, then, Christian purity admits of infinite growth. For I can find no hint in the Bible of a degree of spiritual life in which increasing light will not reveal in us elements of evil unseen before, and I cannot conceive such. Consequently Christian purity admits of no finality. But since Christ is ever ready to save us now from all conscious defilement we may speak of it as offered to us in a certain and very blessed completeness.